Rivers and Streams

Diyan Leake

raintree
a Capstone company — publishers for children

Raintree is an imprint of Capstone Global Library Limited, a company incorporated in England and Wales having its registered office at 7 Pilgrim Street, London, EC4V 6LB – Registered company number: 6695582

www.raintreepublishers.co.uk
myorders@raintreepublishers.co.uk

Text © Capstone Global Library Limited 2015
First published in hardback in 2014
Paperback edition first published in 2015
The moral rights of the proprietor have been asserted.

Edited by Joanna Issa and Penny West
Designed by Philippa Jenkins
Original illustrations © Capstone Global Library Ltd 2014
Picture research by Mica Brancic
Production by Helen McCreath
Originated by Capstone Global Library Ltd
Printed and bound in China

ISBN 978 1 406 28385 3 (hardback)
18 17 16 15 14
10 9 8 7 6 5 4 3 2 1

ISBN 978 1 406 28391 4 (paperback)
19 18 17 16 15
10 9 8 7 6 5 4 3 2 1

British Library Cataloguing in Publication Data
Leake, Diyan
          Rivers and Streams (Water, Water Everywhere!)
A full catalogue record for this book is available from the British Library.

Acknowledgements
We would like to thank the following for permission to reproduce photographs: Alamy pp. 7, 21 (© David Wall), 12, 22c (© Matt Botwood (CStock)), 13 (© John Morrison), 19, 23 (© WoodyStock), 21 (© All Canada Photos); FLPA p. 11 (Ariadne Van Zandbergen); Getty Images pp. 8 (MyLoupe/UIG), 20 (Cultura/Colin Hawkins); Naturepl.com pp. 9, 22b (Robert Thompson); Shutterstock pp. 4 (© Waynelmage), 5 (© Josef Hanus), 6 (© Xavier Marchant), 10 (© Nejron Photo), 15 (© rm), 16 (© Radiokafka), 17, 23a, 23c (© Irina Fischer), 18 (© Frank L Junior).

Cover photograph reproduced with permission of Shutterstock (© Dmitry Naumov).
Back cover photograph reproduced by permission of Shutterstock/© rm.

We would like to thank Michael Bright and Diana Bentley for their invaluable help in the preparation of this book.

Every effort has been made to contact copyright holders of material reproduced in this book. Any omissions will be rectified in subsequent printings if notice is given to the publisher.

All the Internet addresses (URLs) given in this book were valid at the time of going to press. However, due to the dynamic nature of the Internet, some addresses may have changed, or sites may have changed or ceased to exist since publication. While the author and publisher regret any inconvenience this may cause readers, no responsibility for any such changes can be accepted by either the author or the publisher.

Contents

Rivers

This is a river.

Rivers are full of water.

Some rivers flow down to the sea.

mouth

The mouth of the river is where it meets the sea.

A river is like a waterslide.

Many rivers start in high places.

The water flows downhill.

The water flows into the sea.

Streams

Rivers are small at the beginning. They are called streams.

Some streams join together
and become rivers.

Rivers of the world

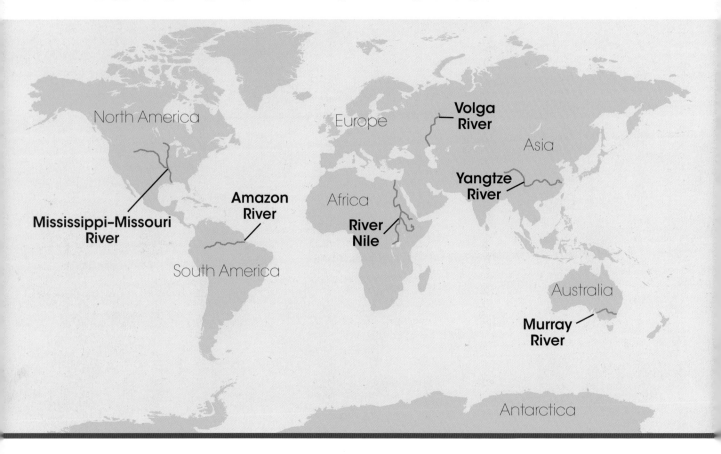

There are rivers all over the world.

The Amazon River is one of
the longest rivers in the world.

15

Boats on rivers

This boat is on a river. It is carrying

people from place to place.

This barge is on a river.
It is carrying a lot of goods.

The power of rivers

There is a lot of energy in the flow of a river. Energy is what we need to make things work.

River energy can be made into energy for our homes. It can be made into light and heat.

Having fun on a river

It is fun to spend time by a river.

Stay safe! Always have an adult with you when you are near water.

Quiz

Which of these shows the mouth of a river?

A

B

C

Answer on page 24

Picture glossary

 **barge** flat-bottomed boat used on canals and rivers to carry goods

 **energy** what we need to make things work

 **goods** things for sale

Index

Answer to quiz on page 22: Picture **A** shows the mouth of a river.

Note to parents and teachers

Before reading

Tell the children you are going to give them a clue about the sort of water they will be learning about next. Play the sound of running water in a river or a stream, using a clip downloaded from the Internet. What sort of water do they think they are going to learn about?

After reading

- Show the children how to make a "mountain" out of damp sand. Simulate rainfall by pouring water onto the top of the mountain. Ask the children to watch and describe what happens. Encourage them to investigate further on their own.

- Re-read pages 18 and 19. Explain that the energy in flowing river water can be harnessed by using a waterwheel. Show photos of waterwheels and water turbines. Help the children to make a simple model waterwheel. Can they use the energy of water flowing from a tap to make the waterwheel turn?